PREPAR

MULTIPLE SKILLS
SERIES: Reading

Third Edition

Richard A. Boning

**SRA
McGraw-Hill**

Columbus, Ohio

A Division of The **McGraw·Hill** Companies

Cover, David Muench/Tony Stone Images

SRA/McGraw-Hill

*A Division of The **McGraw·Hill** Companies*

Printed in the United States of America.

Send all inquiries to:
SRA/McGraw-Hill
8787 Orion Place
Columbus, OH 43240-4027

ISBN 0-02-688404-6

6 7 8 9 BSE 06 05 04 03

PURPOSE

The *Multiple Skills Series* is a nonconsumable reading program designed to develop a cluster of key reading skills and to integrate these skills with each other and with the other language arts. *Multiple Skills* is also diagnostic, making it possible for you to identify specific types of reading skills that might be causing difficulty for individual students.

FOR WHOM

The twelve levels of the *Multiple Skills Series* are geared to students who comprehend on the pre-first- through ninth-grade reading levels.

- The Picture Level is for children who have not acquired a basic sight vocabulary.
- The Preparatory 1 Level is for children who have developed a limited basic sight vocabulary.
- The Preparatory 2 Level is for children who have a basic sight vocabulary but are not yet reading on the first-grade level.
- Books A through I are appropriate for students who can read on grade levels one through nine respectively. Because of their high interest level, the books may also be used effectively with students functioning at these levels of competence in other grades.

The **Multiple Skills Series Placement Tests** will help you determine the appropriate level for each student.

PLACEMENT TESTS

The Elementary Placement Test (for grades Pre-1 through 3) and the Midway Placement Tests (for grades 4–9) will help you place each student properly. The tests consist of representative units selected from the series. The test books contain two forms, X and Y. One form may be used for placement and the second as a posttest to measure progress. The tests are easy to administer and score. Blackline Masters are provided for worksheets and student performance profiles.

THE BOOKS

This third edition of the *Multiple Skills Series* maintains the quality and focus that have distinguished this program for over 25 years. The series includes four books at each level, Picture Level through Level I. Each book in the Picture Level through Level B contains 25 units. Each book in Level C through Level I contains 50 units. The units within each book increase in difficulty. The books within a level also increase in difficulty— Level A, Book 2 is slightly more difficult than Level A, Book 1, and so on. This gradual increase in difficulty permits students to advance from one book to the next and from one level to the next without frustration.

To the Teacher

Each book contains an **About This Book** page, which explains the skills to the students and shows them how to approach reading the selections and questions. In the lowest levels, you should read About This Book to the children.

The questions that follow each unit are designed to develop specific reading skills. In the lowest levels, you should read the questions to the children.

In the Preparatory 1 Level, the question pattern in each unit is

      1. Title (main idea)
      2. Stated detail
      3. Picture clue

The **Language Activity Pages** (LAP) in each level consist of four parts: Exercising Your Skill, Expanding Your Skill, Exploring Language, and Expressing Yourself. These pages lead the students beyond the book through a broadening spiral of writing, speaking, and other individual and group language activities that apply, extend, and integrate the skills being developed. You may use all, some, or none of the activities in any LAP; however, some LAP activities depend on preceding ones. In the lowest levels, you should read the LAPs to the children.

In the Preparatory 1 Level, each set of Language Activity Pages focuses on a particular skill developed through the book:

First LAP	Details
Second LAP	Picture interpretations
Third LAP	Details with some picture interpretations
Last LAP	Main ideas

SESSIONS

The *Multiple Skills Series* is an individualized reading program that may be used with small groups or an entire class. Short sessions are the most effective. Use a short session every day or every other day, completing a few units in each session. Time allocated to the Language Activity Pages depends on the abilities of the individual students.

SCORING

Students should record their answers on the reproducible worksheets. The worksheets make scoring easier and provide uniform records of the children's work. Using worksheets also avoids consuming the books.

Because it is important for the students to know how they are progressing, you should score the units as soon as they've been completed. Then you can discuss the questions and activities with the students and encourage them to justify their responses. Many of the LAPs are open-ended and do not lend themselves to an objective score; for this reason, there are no answer keys for these pages.

When you read a story, you read words and sentences that belong together. They all help to tell about one **main idea**. Read this story. Think about what it is mainly about.

> Jon has a lot of pets. He has a cat. He has a dog. He has a fish, too.

Do all of the sentences in the story tell about Jon's pets? Would "Jon's Pets" be a good name for the story? Figuring out what a story is mainly about is important in reading.

In reading we also need to remember the **facts**. The facts are the things a story tells. In the story above, what was the boy's name? What pets did he have? A good reader pays attention to the facts.

Sometimes a story has a **picture** to go with it. The picture may tell you some things that the words do not. The picture can help tell the story.

In this book, you will read stories and look at pictures. After you have read a story and looked at the picture, choose a **title**, or name, that tells what the story is mainly about. Then answer questions about the facts in the story and in the picture.

"Do you want a ride?" asked Father. Dick said no. He would walk home with his friends. Father went home in the car. Dick began to walk with his friends.

1. The best title is—

   (A) Dick Walks Home

   (B) Dick Helps Father

2. Dick went home with his—

   (A) sister

   (B) friends

3. In the picture, the boy is—

   (A) talking

   (B) riding

"I hear a baby crying," said Betty. Betty looked and looked. At last she found what was crying. It was not a baby. It was a kitten.

1. The best title is—

    (A) Betty Finds a Lost Toy

    (B) Betty Hears Something

2. Betty found a—

    (A) kitten

    (B) dog

3. In the picture, you can see a—

    (A) hat

    (B) house

Ann and Pat like to dance. "I want to dance and dance," said Ann. "I will work and work." Ann and Pat worked and worked. They danced and danced.

1. The best title is—

   (A) Ann and Pat Paint

   (B) Ann and Pat Dance

2. Ann and Pat—

   (A) worked

   (B) washed a car

3. In the picture, you can see a—

   (A) bar

   (B) wagon

Mother and Fred were going for a ride. "May my new friend come too?" asked Fred. Mother said yes. Mother, Fred, and his new friend went for a long ride.

1. The best title is—

   (A) Going for a Ride

   (B) A New Car

2. Fred had—

   (A) an old friend

   (B) a new friend

3. In the picture, you can see a—

   (A) hat

   (B) cat

Father wanted a balloon for Jane. But he did not know what balloon to get. There were red balloons, yellow balloons, and green balloons. Father got a red balloon.

1. The best title is—

   (A) Jane Has a Birthday Party

   (B) Father Gets a Balloon for Jane

2. Father got a—

   (A) yellow balloon

   (B) red balloon

3. In the picture, you can see—

   (A) trees

   (B) cars

Dom looked out the window. He saw his mother coming from the store. She had many bags of food. Dom went out to help her.

1. The best title is—

   (A) Dom Helps His Mother

   (B) Dom Goes Out to Play

2. Dom's mother had bags of—

   (A) toys

   (B) food

3. In the picture, the boy is—

   (A) eating

   (B) running

A. Exercising Your Skill

Look at the picture. Answer the questions.

1. Who is in the picture?

2. What is the girl looking at?

3. Where is the girl?

B. Expanding Your Skill

With your classmates, think of some questions you can ask about the picture in Part A.

What words do your questions begin with? On your paper, make a list of words you can use when asking questions.

C. Exploring Language

Read or listen to the story. Then answer the questions.

Rosa has a black kitten named Boots. One day, Boots ran behind a chair. She didn't come out...and didn't come out...and didn't come out.

Finally, she ran back out. She carried a pretty red ribbon in her mouth.

"Oh, Boots!" cried Rosa. "My hair ribbon has been lost for days. Thank you for finding it."

1. How many animals are in the story?
   one   two   three

2. What is a baby cat called?
   a kitten   a bean   a puppy

3. What is the name of Boots' owner?
   Boots   Twinkle Toes   Rosa

D. Expressing Yourself

Tell the class a story about a pet. Then ask questions. See if your classmates remember your story.

"Look in the basket and you will see your birthday surprise," said Mother. Mary looked in the basket. There was a little dog. Mary was happy.

1.   The best title is—

   (A) Mother and Mary Go Away

   (B) Mary Likes Her Surprise

2.   Mary's surprise was a—

   (A) dog

   (B) cat

3.   In the picture, you can see a—

   (A) basket

   (B) cat

Mother wanted the children to help her. The children wanted to play some more. Mother said, "You have played all day. Now it is time to work."

1. The best title is—

   (A) Time to Work

   (B) A New Game

2. The children wanted—

   (A) to sleep

   (B) to play

3. In the picture, there are—

   (A) two girls

   (B) three trees

Bill, Mother, and Father went out to eat. They went to eat fish. Bill got some fish. Mother and Father got some fish too. They had a good time.

1. The best title is—

    (A) Eating Fish

    (B) Playing Games

2. Bill, Mother, and Father are—

    (A) at home

    (B) out

3. In the picture, you can see a—

    (A) dog

    (B) fish

There were two horses at the farm. One was brown and one was white. Jill said, "I take care of the brown horse. Father takes care of the white one."

1. The best title is—

   (A) A Horse Runs Away

   (B) The Horses at the Farm

2. Jill takes care of the—

   (A) brown horse

   (B) white horse

3. In the picture, the girl is—

   (A) in a school

   (B) at a farm

The children made a big picture. They worked for three days. The picture showed water. The picture showed plants. The picture showed animals.

1. The best title is—

    (A) The Children Go to School

    (B) The Children Make a Picture

2. The picture shows—

    (A) toys and books

    (B) plants and animals

3. In the picture, you can see—

    (A) three children

    (B) two children

"The store is far away," said Ann. "May I ride my bike?" Mother said Ann could ride her bike, but she must look out for the cars.

1. The best title is—

   (A) Ann Can Ride to the Store

   (B) Ann Finds Her Old Bike

2. Mother told Ann to look out for—

   (A) trains

   (B) cars

3. In the picture, the girl is—

   (A) talking

   (B) riding

A. Exercising Your Skill

Look at the picture. Then answer the questions.

1. What is the girl doing?

2. What is she wearing?

3. Is she happy or sad? How do you know?

B. Expanding Your Skill

Think about the girl in the picture. Where might the girl be going? With your class, list places the girl might go. Think about these places.

- a fun place
- a quiet place
- a busy place
- a scary place
- a noisy place
- an empty place

C. Exploring Language

Read the words in the box. On your own paper, write the words that tell about things you see in the picture in Part A.

tree	house	lion	road
table	moon	bike	ring

Now use the words on your paper to finish these sentences.

1. Cars go on the ____ .
2. A bird sat in the ____ .
3. My new red ____ goes fast.
4. The girl lives in a ____ .

D. Expressing Yourself

Do one of these things.

1. Draw a picture of yourself in your favorite place. Trade pictures with a classmate. Think of a title for your classmate's picture.

2. Tell the class a story about a day when you rode a bike. Instead, you may tell about a special walk you took.

Fred said, "I worked a long time. I worked all night. Now I am going to sleep." Fred went to bed. He did not get up for a long time.

1. The best title is—

   (A) Fred Goes to Work

   (B) Fred Goes to Bed

2. Fred did not get up for—

   (A) a long time

   (B) three days

3. In the picture, there is a—

   (A) kitten

   (B) dog

"I want a pet," said Maka, "but I do not want a dog or a cat." Grandfather asked what Maka wanted for a pet. Maka said that she wanted a bird.

1. The best title is—

    (A) Maka Finds a Lost Dog

    (B) Maka Wants a Pet

2. Maka wanted a—

    (A) dog

    (B) bird

3. In the picture, you see a—

    (A) truck

    (B) car

"Read us a story," asked the children.
Father began to read. The story was funny.
The children laughed and laughed. The
children asked Father to read one more story.

1. The best title is—

    (A) Father Reads a Funny Story

    (B) The Children Find a Book

2. The children asked Father—

    (A) to stop reading stories

    (B) to read one more story

3. In the picture, the children are—

    (A) sitting

    (B) sleeping

"Come and see my baby sister," said Betty. "She can walk!" Jim went to see the baby. The baby was little but she could walk. She was walking around the house.

1. The best title is—

   (A) The Baby Can Walk

   (B) Betty Plays with the Baby

2. Betty asked Jim to come and see her—

   (A) house

   (B) sister

3. In the picture, you can see a—

   (A) baby

   (B) boy

A man called to talk to Don's father. Don said, "My father is not home. Do you want to talk to my mother?" The man said no. He would call the next day.

1. The best title is—

   (A) Father and a Friend Go Away

   (B) A Call for Don's Father

2. Don said that his father was—

   (A) not home

   (B) in bed

3. In the picture, the boy is—

   (A) talking

   (B) playing

Pat got a pet duck. Mother asked what she was going to call it. Pat said that the duck looked funny when it walked. So she called it "Funny Feet."

1. The best title is—

   (A) A Duck Gets Wet

   (B) Pat's New Pet

2. Pat called her pet—

   (A) Little Duck

   (B) Funny Feet

3. In the picture, you can see—

   (A) a hat

   (B) books

Tom said, "I want to catch a big fish." He got into his boat and went out on the water. He stopped the boat. Soon he had a fish. It was a big fish.

1. The best title is—

   (A) Tom Goes Fishing

   (B) Tom Makes a Boat

2. Tom wanted to catch a—

   (A) little fish

   (B) big fish

3. In the picture, the boy is—

   (A) riding

   (B) standing

A. Exercising Your Skill

Read or listen to the story and answer the questions.

Marty woke up in the middle of the night. The room was dark. Marty's feet were cold. He felt on the floor for his slippers. Then he put them on and climbed back in bed.

In the morning, Marty woke up and walked sleepily out of his room. His sister, Jill, laughed when she saw Marty. "If you are going to a party, you had better get out of your pajamas," she said.

Marty looked down. There on his feet were his best shoes!

1. How many people are in this story?
2. What was cold?
3. Why did Marty put on his best shoes?

B. Expanding Your Skill

Work with a partner. Decide who will be Marty and who will be a reporter. The "reporter" should ask Marty what happened to him in the middle of the night.

C. Exploring Language

Listen to each sentence. Then, on your paper, write **yes** or **no** to answer each question. Be ready to tell why you said **yes** or **no**.

1. Darlene is going to school on a cold, snowy day. Will she wear sandals?
2. Maggie is playing tennis today. Will she wear slippers?
3. Sam is going to a party tonight. Will he wear his best shoes?
4. Mike is swimming in the pool. Is he wearing socks?

Talk about your answers with your class. Tell why you wrote the answers you did.

D. Expressing Yourself

Choose a partner. Have a race to see who in your classroom can count these things faster.

1. the number of white socks
2. the number of shoe laces
3. the number of black shoes

Dick said, "It is too cold to watch the game. I am going home. We can see the game on TV." Jill said she was cold, too. The children went home.

1. The best title is—

   (A) A Cold Day

   (B) A Good Game

2. The children went—

   (A) to a store

   (B) home

3. In the picture, you can see—

   (A) dogs

   (B) coats

"May I take my new book to school?" asked Maria. "I want to show it to my friends." Father said that Maria could take her book to school.

1. The best title is—

    (A) Father Reads a Funny Story

    (B) Maria's New Book

2. Maria's book is—

    (A) old

    (B) new

3. In the picture, you can see—

    (A) food

    (B) books

"What is in the box?" asked Bill. Father said it was a surprise for Bill. Bill looked into the box. The surprise was a new hat.

1. The best title is—

    (A) A Surprise for Bill

    (B) Bill Gets a New Ball

2. Bill's surprise was a—

    (A) hat

    (B) coat

3. In the picture, the boy is—

    (A) reading

    (B) looking

Ann wanted to stay at the zoo. Mother said they could not stay. It was time to go home. Ann went home with Mother, but she was not happy.

1. The best title is—

 (A) Mother and Ann Go to a Show

 (B) Ann Wants to Stay at the Zoo

2. Mother said it was time to go—

 (A) home

 (B) to school

3. In the picture, you can see—

 (A) an animal

 (B) a car

Mother works on a train. The train is very big. Mother makes the train go. The train goes to places all day. Then Mother goes home.

1. The best title is—

   (A) Mother Works on a Train

   (B) Mother Works at Home

2. The train is very—

   (A) big

   (B) little

3. In the picture, you can see a—

   (A) pet

   (B) man

"Put away your toys," called Mother. "It is going to rain." Jane put her toys away. She did not want them to get wet when it rained.

1. The best title is—

   (A) Jane Puts Her Toys Away

   (B) Jane Gets a New Toy

2. Jane did not want her toys—

   (A) to fall

   (B) to get wet

3. In the picture, you can see—

   (A) grass

   (B) a book

A. Exercising Your Skill

Read or listen to the story. Then answer the questions.

Lisa brought a flash light. Linda came with a tent. She carried a blanket over her shoulder.

The friends set up the tent in Lisa's yard. They put the blanket inside and lay down. They told each other funny stories. Then they went to sleep.

- What is the story about?
- What do the friends like to do?
- What is a good title for this story?

B. Expanding Your Skill

Choose a partner. Tell your partner a short story about the first time you did something that you liked a lot. Ask your partner to make up a title for your story.

C. Exploring Language

On your paper, write the letter of the word that finishes each sentence correctly.

1. A story about daisies and roses could be called "The First Time I Picked _____ ."

2. A story about pitchers and home runs could be called "The First Time I Played _____ ."

3. A story about tigers and zebras could be called "The First Time I Went to a _____ ."

D. Expressing Yourself

Think of something you can pretend to be. Tell the class what you are like. Do not tell what you are. See who can guess what you are. (Example: I am round. I am red. I taste good in pie. I am an _____ .)